THE POWER GIFTS

Michael E.B. Maher

Unless otherwise indicated, all Scripture quotations in this teaching are from the *New King James Version* of the bible.

Revised 2021

ISBN: 978-1521765364

Books by Michael E.B. Maher

Foundation Doctrines of Christ

Repentance from Dead Works
Faith toward God
Doctrine of Baptisms
Laying on of Hands
Resurrection of the Dead
Eternal Judgement

Man, the Image of God

The Will of Man
The Spirit of Man
The Conscience of Man
The Mind of Man
The Body of Man

Gifts of the Church

Spiritual Gifts
Ministry Gifts
The Revelation Gifts
The Power Gifts
The Speaking Gifts

End of the Ages

The Last Days
The Seventh Seal
The Millennial Kingdom
The End of the Age

Standalone

There is Sin to Death
Prayer
Being Unforgiving
Being led by the Spirit
Born Free from Sin
The Two Gospels Explained
Being led by the Spirit
Of such is the Kingdom
Rich through His Poverty
Suffering as a Christian
Growing Strong in Spirit
The Believer's Authority in the Earth
The Prayer of Faith
Predestined to His Purpose
Holy Spirit Encounters
The Bible Creation Account
The Blood of Christ
The Church and the State

Contents

Chapter 1 1
The power of God 1
The tangible power of God 1
Chapter 2 5
Special faith 5
Differing levels of faith 5
Purpose of this gift 12
Scriptural examples 12
Guidelines for this gift 17
Chapter 3 21
Gifts of healings 21
Healing by faith 21
Healing by the anointing 25
Purpose of this gift 27
Scriptural examples 28
Guidelines for this gift 33
Chapter 4 39
The working of miracles 39
Miracles defined 39
Miracles by faith 43
Miracles by the anointing 46
Purpose of this gift 47
Scriptural examples 48

Guidelines for this gift 51

Chapter 1
The power of God

The tangible power of God

1 Corinthians 12:7-10 "But the manifestation of the Spirit is given to each one for the profit of all: (8) for to one is given the word of wisdom through the Spirit, to another the word of knowledge through the same Spirit, (9) to another faith by the same Spirit, to another gifts of healings by the same Spirit, (10) to another the working of miracles, to another prophecy, to another discerning of spirits, to another different kinds of tongues, to another the interpretation of tongues."

As one can see in the above quoted passage of scripture there are nine listed gifts of the Holy Spirit. As we study the gifts of the Spirit we will see that the nine gifts can be consolidated into three different categories. The reason that they can be consolidated into these categories is because each of the gifts categorized do something similar. The first of the three categories are what we call the revelation gifts. The reason we call them the revelation gifts is because the Holy Spirit reveals something through each one of these gifts. The gifts that fall into this category are; the word of wisdom, the word of knowledge, and the discerning of spirits. The second of the three categories are what we call the power gifts. The reason we call them the power gifts is because the Holy Spirit demonstrates His

The power of God

power through each one of these gifts. The gifts that fall into this category are; special faith, gifts of healings, and the working of miracles. It is this category of gifts that we will be studying in this book. The third of the three categories are what we call the speaking gifts. The reason we call them the speaking gifts is because the Holy Spirit speaks to the church through each one of these gifts. The gifts that fall into this category are; prophecy, different kinds of tongues, and the interpretation of tongues.

> *Acts 1:8 "But you shall receive power when the Holy Spirit has come upon you; and you shall be witnesses to Me in Jerusalem, and in all Judea and Samaria, and to the end of the earth."*

God's power is real and it can be tangible. The apostle Paul made a very simple yet profound statement, when he said that the kingdom of God is not in word but in power (1 Corinthians 4:20). Nevertheless even though Paul's statement is completely true, most believers only know the word of God and have never encountered His tangible power. So why is that? The reason is because the only miracle most believers have experienced is the miracle of the new birth. The miracle of the new birth takes place in the spirit realm however, and very seldom is there any tangible manifestation of God's power that the individual experiences when they are saved. In the above quoted passage of scripture the Lord Jesus has taught the church that they will be exposed to the power of God when they experience the baptism of the Holy Spirit. Sadly a large portion of the church today, for various reasons, have not experienced the baptism of the Holy Spirit, and have therefore not been exposed to God's power.

The power of God

1 Corinthians 2:4-5 "And my speech and my preaching were not with persuasive words of human wisdom, but in demonstration of the Spirit and of power, (5) that your faith should not be in the wisdom of men but in the power of God."

Unlike the church today, the saints in the early church were fully acquainted with the power of God. So why is that? The reason is because they were exposed to God's power the moment they came into the kingdom. In the above quoted passage of scripture the apostle Paul teaches us that he demonstrated God's power in every church that he planted. So why did Paul deem it necessary to expose the saints to God's power right from the outset? Some would have us to believe that Paul did that so that he could establish his credentials as an apostle, so that the church would accept his letters as being authoritative scripture. Those who teach such foolishness are the same people who deny the power of God in the church today. Nevertheless Paul teaches us in this passage that the reason he exposed the saints to God's power, was so that they could learn to place their faith in His power and not in the wisdom of man's words. Sadly much of the church today practices this passage of scripture in reverse, for their faith lies in the wisdom of mans words and not in the power of God. Nevertheless as we will see in this book, the New Testament pattern for the church is to experience God's tangible power demonstrated in their midst through the various gifts of the Spirit, particularly the power gifts of special faith, gifts of healings and working of miracles.

The power of God

Chapter 2
Special faith

Differing levels of faith

Romans 4:19-22 "And not being weak in faith, he did not consider his own body, already dead (since he was about a hundred years old), and the deadness of Sarah's womb. (20) He did not waver at the promise of God through unbelief, but was strengthened in faith, giving glory to God, (21) and being fully convinced that what He had promised He was also able to perform. (22) And therefore "It was accounted to him for righteousness."

In this book we will look at each of the power gifts in turn so that we can more clearly understand how each gift operates. The first gift listed as part of the power gifts is called the gift of faith. Before we can discuss this particular gift however, we first need to understand two spiritual truths about faith. The first truth that we need to understand is how faith works, and the second truth we need to understand is that the New Testament teaches us that there are in fact three different levels of faith. And so the first spiritual truth which we will discuss is just how faith works. God endows every human being born into the earth with the gift of faith, and that faith resides in the mind of man. It is because all men are endowed with the gift of faith that children have what is often referred to as childlike faith (Mark 9:42). Because faith is part of the DNA (so to speak) of every human being, everyone (without

Special faith

exception) believes something. Nevertheless the faith given by God was always intended primarily for the individual to be able to appropriate the promises of God in their lives, including the promise of salvation through Jesus Christ. So how does an individual exercise the faith that resides in their minds? In the above quoted passage of scripture the apostle Paul uses Abraham as an example to teach us about that concept. The context of the above example is that God had given Abraham His word that he and Sarah would have a son in their old age. And so we see that the first step in exercising our faith is that God must reveal his word (promise) to us. In other words God must give us understanding of His word. For example, because God does not give certain unbelievers understanding of the gospel of salvation, they cannot exercise their faith to be saved (Mark 4:11-12). Paul then goes on to teach us in this passage that Abraham became fully convinced that God could do what He had promised. In other words Abraham became fully convinced in his mind that God's word was true (Romans 14:5). Some will ask the question what it means to be fully convinced in one's mind about the truthfulness of God's word. It simply means that all doubt is removed, and so whereas the individual may have been in two minds about a subject before, they have now become single minded on the subject i.e. they are now fully convinced in their minds (James 1:6-8). And so we see that the second step in exercising our faith is to renew our thinking to become fully convinced about the truthfulness of God's word on a particular subject. To become fully convinced in our minds as to the truthfulness of God's word is the same thing as believing in His word. When that happens the saint's thinking becomes fully focused on the reality of God's word to the exclusion of the natural reality of their circumstances. In the above example we see that Abraham

Special faith

no longer considered either his or Sarah's physical conditions and became completely focused on what God had said on the subject. And so we see that it is only when we are fully convinced in our minds that our faith is then finally activated. Some get to this point however and go no further. For example, when Jesus walked in the flesh there were many scribes in Judea who believed (i.e. they were fully convinced) that He was the Messiah, but the scripture teaches us that they did not confess Him because they feared the Jews and didn't want to give up their places in the Jewish synagogues (John 12:42-43). In other words they chose not to act on that which they believed. And so we see that the third and final step in exercising our faith is to make the wilful decision to act on that which we believe. The apostle Paul cautions the saints in this area however, for he warns us not to act before we are fully convinced, because to do so would not be an act of faith and in fact those actions would be considered sinful (Romans 14:23). Nevertheless for those saints who are fully convinced, the next step is to act on that which they believe. The apostle James put it this way, "by works (our actions) faith is made perfect (or complete)" (James 2:22). It is only when our faith is completed i.e. fully exercised, that it releases the power of God which transforms our natural circumstances to line up with the reality of God's word. In other words our circumstances are changed to conform to God's word. And so we see that when Abraham and Sarah finally acted on God's word, Isaac was conceived.

> *Ephesians 2:8 "For by grace you have been saved through faith and that not of yourselves; it is the gift of God."*

Special faith

The second spiritual truth which we will discuss is the fact that the New Testament teaches us that there are three different levels of faith. The first level of faith is the faith which, as we have already mentioned, is given to every human being, and it is this faith which enables people to believe the gospel and thus be saved. In the scripture quoted above the apostle Paul confirms the truth to us that this faith is a gift from God. Because people need this level of faith in order to be saved, some have referred to it as saving faith. Nevertheless even though every human being has been given this level of faith not everyone is saved. So why is that? The answer is because one can only apply one's faith in that which they understand, and because certain unbelievers do not understand the gospel they cannot therefore exercise their faith in the gospel and thus be saved (Matthew 13:19).

Romans 1:16-17 "For I am not ashamed of the gospel of Christ, for it is the power of God to salvation for everyone who believes, for the Jew first and also for the Greek. (17) For in it the righteousness of God is revealed from faith to faith; as it is written, "The just shall live by faith."

The faith that is given to the saints to believe in the gospel and thus be saved is that same faith that the saints are required to use in order to live the godly lifestyles that God has called us to live. The apostle Paul talks about this level of faith in the above quoted passage of scripture, when he tells us that the saints (the just) are to live by faith. Because saints need this level of faith in order to live their Christian lives, some have referred to it as daily living faith. Nevertheless which ever term you give it, i.e. saving faith or daily living faith, it is still the basic level of faith that is

Special faith

given equally to every saint to firstly, believe the gospel, and secondly to live the godly lifestyles that God expects His children to live. Because faith is directly related to our understanding, the saints are able to grow in their faith as their level of understanding of God's word increases. And so we see that every believer comes into the kingdom of God with the exact same level of faith i.e. they all believe the gospel of salvation. Nevertheless some believers continue to grow in their faith because they continue to grow in their understanding of God's word, and are thus able to exercise their faith in more and more of His word. Many believers never grow in faith however, simply because they never grow in their understanding of God's word beyond the gospel message of salvation in Christ Jesus.

> *Romans 12:3-7 "For I say, through the grace given to me, to everyone who is among you, not to think of himself more highly than he ought to think, but to think soberly, as God has dealt to each one a measure of faith. (4) For as we have many members in one body, but all the members do not have the same function, (5) so we, being many, are one body in Christ, and individually members of one another. (6) Having then gifts differing according to the grace that is given to us, let us use them: if prophecy, let us prophesy in proportion to our faith; (7) or ministry, let us use it in our ministering; he who teaches, in teaching."*

The second level of faith which we will discuss is the faith which is imparted to each member of the body of Christ when they come into the kingdom of God. When believers are born-again God imparts an additional measure of faith to the individual, which allows them to

Special faith

operate in the gifting that they have received in the body of Christ. In the passage of scripture quoted above the apostle Paul teaches us that each of us has received a specific gift that dictates our function in the body of Christ. Paul goes on to say in this passage that each gift is accompanied by its own measure of faith. To further explain this concept Paul goes on to give the example of those who prophesy, by telling us that they should prophesy in proportion to the faith that they have received. And so we see that because this faith is directly related to the ministry gift that each saint receives, some have referred to this faith as ministry gift faith. In the same passage Paul teaches us to think of ourselves in line with the measure of faith that God has given each one of us. Obviously he is implying that some have received more faith than others, depending on the functional gift that they have received in the body of Christ. So how does ministry gift faith differ from our daily living faith? Earlier we discussed the concept of our faith in God's word being directly related to our understanding of His word. And we also established that unless God gives us understanding of His word that it remains hidden from us (1 Corinthians 2:7). Therefore when God imparts a gift to His saint He also gives them spiritual understanding on how to operate in their gift. And because they have that understanding they are able to exercise their faith to operate in their gift. For example one who has received the gift of pastor receives spiritual understanding on how to operate as a pastor, because of which they are therefore able to exercise their faith to operate in that gift. This same principle applies in reverse however. For example one who receives the gift of evangelist does not receive spiritual understanding on how to operate as a pastor, because of which they are therefore unable to exercise their faith to operate in the gift of pastor. Therefore each member in the

Special faith

body has been given a specific function, and one who has been called to function as an ear cannot function as an eye (1 Corinthians 12:17-18). Therefore the principle of ministry gift faith is that just as God in His sovereignty imparts the gift to the individual, so it is that He only imparts understanding about the gift to the one who has received the gift. And so we can see that although the saints can grow in their daily living faith as the Lord opens their understanding to His word, daily living faith can never be used to operate in ministry gifts because God only opens our understanding to the ministry gifts which He has given us.

1 Corinthians 12:7-9 "But the manifestation of the Spirit is given to each one for the profit of all: (8) for to one is given the word of wisdom through the Spirit, to another the word of knowledge through the same Spirit, (9) to another faith by the same Spirit, to another gifts of healings by the same Spirit."

The third and final level of faith which we will discuss is the gift of special faith which is mentioned in the above quoted passage of scripture. It is this faith which is the subject of this book, and so we will obviously examine this level of faith in detail in this chapter. For the purposes of our discussion in this section however, we will briefly differentiate between this spiritual gift of faith and the other two levels of faith that we have already mentioned, i.e. daily living faith and ministry gift faith. The simplest way to explain the difference between the above mentioned gift of faith and the other two is that this faith is in fact the faith of the Holy Spirit. In this passage the apostle Paul declares that when these gifts are manifested in the church that it is in fact the Holy Spirit that is manifesting Himself through

Special faith

each one of these gifts, which would obviously include the gift of faith. And so whereas the other two levels of faith that we have already discussed are the faiths given to the saints by God, this faith is in fact God's faith being displayed through the one being used by the Holy Spirit at the time. As we examine various scriptural examples of this gift of faith in operation later in this chapter, this truth will become a lot clearer to understand.

Purpose of this gift

1 Corinthians 12:7-9 "But the manifestation of the Spirit is given to each one for the profit of all: (8) for to one is given the word of wisdom through the Spirit, to another the word of knowledge through the same Spirit, (9) to another faith by the same Spirit."

One way of explaining the gift of (special) faith is that God supernaturally endows the individual with His faith, resulting in the person in that instant becoming "another man". God does that when He chooses to intervene in the affairs of men through the demonstration of His power in the earth. And so invariably this gift is linked to either the working of miracles or gifts of healings, for both of those gifts also demonstrate God's power. Because God's power is released through the operation of this gift it always glorifies the Lord, as those who witness the resulting miracle recognize that God's power has been manifested.

Scriptural examples

Special faith

1 Kings 18:36-40 "And it came to pass, at the time of the offering of the evening sacrifice, that Elijah the prophet came near and said, "Lord God of Abraham, Isaac, and Israel, let it be known this day that You are God in Israel and I am Your servant, and that I have done all these things at Your word. (37) Hear me, O Lord, hear me, that this people may know that You are the Lord God, and that You have turned their hearts back to You again." (38) Then the fire of the Lord fell and consumed the burnt sacrifice, and the wood and the stones and the dust, and it licked up the water that was in the trench. (39) Now when all the people saw it, they fell on their faces; and they said, "The Lord, He is God! The Lord, He is God!" (40) And Elijah said to them, "Seize the prophets of Baal! Do not let one of them escape!" So they seized them; and Elijah brought them down to the Brook Kishon and executed them there."

As we look at biblical examples of the gift of special faith it will become clearer as to just how this gift operates. The first example that we will discuss is recorded in the above quoted passage of scripture where we see the prophet Elijah operating in the gift of special faith. In this account Elijah called fire down from heaven in the sight of all of Israel. The context of this account is that displaying great boldness (faith), Elijah had challenged the prophets of Baal in front of the whole nation. His challenge was that he and the prophets of Baal should each offer the sacrifice of a bull on an altar and call upon their God to answer by fire, and the one who answered by fire would be declared to be the true God of Israel. The Israelites enthusiastically approved of the challenge, and so much to the trepidation of the prophets of Baal they were forced to accept Elijah's

Special faith

challenge. Elijah allowed the prophets of Baal to offer their sacrifice first, and so they called on their god the whole day, with much crying out, prophesying and ritually cutting themselves until their blood flowed freely, but nothing happened (1 Kings 18:1-35). And so we pick up the account at the end of the day when Elijah offered his sacrifice and called upon the Lord. This account reveals that God answered Elijah by fire, which consumed not only the sacrifice but the altar as well. The moment God did that, Elijah commanded the Israelites to kill the prophets of Baal. When we read the rest of this account in scripture it becomes very clear that on this occasion Elijah was operating in the gift of special faith. So how do we know that? We know that because the very next day, when Elijah heard that Jezebel the Queen had threatened to kill him in retaliation for the killing of her prophets, that instead of confronting her in faith as he had done with the prophets of Baal the previous day, Elijah ran for his life (1 Kings 19:1-3). So why did Elijah run? The reason is because the anointing of special faith had lifted off of him and he was now operating in his own daily living faith, which clearly was not up to the task of taking on Queen Jezebel. Obviously even Elijah's ministry gift faith as a prophet was not up to the task, for had it been, he would have stood his ground and not fled. In other words when God imparted to Elijah the gift of special faith he became "another man".

Acts 3:1-8 "Now Peter and John went up together to the temple at the hour of prayer, the ninth hour. (2) And a certain man lame from his mother's womb was carried, whom they laid daily at the gate of the temple which is called Beautiful, to ask alms from those who entered the temple; (3) who, seeing Peter and John about to go into the temple, asked for alms.

Special faith

(4) And fixing his eyes on him, with John, Peter said, "Look at us." (5) So, he gave them his attention, expecting to receive something from them. (6) Then Peter said, "Silver and gold I do not have, but what I do have I give you: In the name of Jesus Christ of Nazareth, rise up and walk." (7) And he took him by the right hand and lifted him up, and immediately his feet and ankle bones received strength. (8) So, he, leaping up, stood and walked and entered the temple with them--walking, leaping, and praising God."

The next example which we will discuss is recorded in the above quoted passage of scripture, where we see this gift manifesting itself through the ministry of the apostle Peter. In this account Peter miraculously healed a lame man in front of everyone in the temple. It is important to note that in the context of this account Peter had walked past this man on many occasions before this incident, for the scripture tells us that he was laid daily at this gate. And so Peter would have walked past this man every time he went to the temple, but at no stage before this incident did Peter make any attempt to pray for his healing, even though clearly this man had very probably asked alms from Peter before and Peter may have even given him alms from time to time. However on this occasion something different happened, for the scripture says that Peter fixed his eyes on the man. So what caused Peter to focus his full attention on the man on this occasion? The reason was the anointing of the Holy Spirit coming upon Peter to operate in the gift of special faith. When that happened a spirit of boldness rose up in Peter and he knew that he had the faith to heal that man. The gift of special faith can be equated to a spirit of boldness because the one through whom this faith is manifested knows no doubt, for it is the faith of the Holy

Special faith

Spirit Himself. And so Peter, in this spirit of boldness, spoke the word of God to that man and acted on that word by pulling this man up off the ground. The moment Peter did that the power of God was released and miraculously healed the man. And so we see that it was neither Peter's daily living faith, nor his ministry gift faith as an apostle, that healed this man because if it had been he would have healed this man long before this occasion. It also wasn't the lame man's faith that caused this miracle to take place because he was expecting to receive alms from Peter, not his healing. This incident is recorded in scripture as a clear example of the manifestation of the gift of special faith.

> *Acts 13:6-12 "Now when they had gone through the island to Paphos, they found a certain sorcerer, a false prophet, a Jew whose name was Bar-Jesus, (7) who was with the proconsul, Sergius Paulus, an intelligent man. This man called for Barnabas and Saul and sought to hear the word of God. (8) But Elymas the sorcerer (for so his name is translated) withstood them, seeking to turn the proconsul away from the faith. (9) Then Saul, who also is called Paul, filled with the Holy Spirit, looked intently at him (10) and said, "O full of all deceit and all fraud, you son of the devil, you enemy of all righteousness, will you not cease perverting the straight ways of the Lord? (11) And now, indeed, the hand of the Lord is upon you, and you shall be blind, not seeing the sun for a time." And immediately a dark mist fell on him, and he went around seeking someone to lead him by the hand. (12) Then the proconsul believed, when he saw what had been done, being astonished at the teaching of the Lord."*

Special faith

The above quoted account in scripture is another example of the gift of special faith in operation, this time through the ministry of the apostle Paul. The scripture tells us plainly on this occasion that the anointing of the Holy Spirit came upon Paul, for the scripture says that Paul was filled with the Holy Spirit. And so in response to that anointing coming upon Paul he became fully focused on Elymas the sorcerer, for the scripture says that Paul looked intently at him (almost the same language used to describe Peter fixing his eyes on the lame man we discussed earlier). And so just like Peter, Paul on this occasion boldly proclaimed God's word to Elymas and the moment that happened God's power was released and Elymas became blind. This was neither Paul's daily living faith nor his ministry gift faith as an apostle being displayed on this occasion, for had it been Paul's faith he would have used it to deal with many other similar incidents that he encountered throughout his ministry. This is the only occasion recorded however, where Paul responded in such a manner to his adversaries when he preached the gospel. On all other occasions Paul either walked away or was chased out or was even physically attacked by those who opposed his message. Clearly this incident is recorded in scripture as another example of the manifestation of the gift of special faith, or more correctly stated the faith of the Holy Spirit. And so we see that in all three accounts that we have looked at in this section we can clearly see that the faith displayed through these men at the time was not their own, it was a demonstration of the gift of special faith.

Guidelines for this gift

Special faith

1 Samuel 10:6 "Then the Spirit of the Lord will come upon you, and you will prophesy with them and be turned into another man."

In the examples which we discussed in the previous section, we saw that the Holy Spirit described both the apostles Peter and Paul becoming fully focused to the exclusion of anything else when the anointing came on them. In the above quoted passage of scripture the Holy Spirit gives us a bit more insight as to why individuals become so focused when they operate in the gift of faith. The context of this passage is that Samuel the prophet was prophesying to Saul as to what would happen to him as he journeyed back home. In this passage Samuel tells Saul that when the Spirit of the Lord came upon him that he would be turned into another man. Although Samuel is referring to the gift of prophecy in this passage, the principle remains the same for the gift of faith, i.e. one who operates in the gift of faith turns into another man when the anointing comes upon them, because at that moment they are filled with the faith of the Holy Spirit. As with all the spiritual gifts, the gift of faith is only manifested as and when the Holy Spirit chooses. In other words one who has received this gift cannot operate in it at will; they can only make themselves available to the Holy Spirit to be used by Him when He chooses to do so.

I will end this chapter with an example of this gift being made manifest through my ministry. I used to play squash, and I was what you would call a very average player. I had a friend that I used to play squash with from time to time, and he was a league player. As you can imagine our games were never equal, and he used to always soundly beat me. On a good day, I would only ever get a couple of points off of him in our encounters, but I used to

Special faith

enjoy the challenge anyway. He was an unbeliever and he knew that I was a Christian. I had witnessed to him on occasions but he was not interested, and always viewed my faith as a bit strange. One day on the squash court he insisted on telling me a joke that he had heard. I said that he could share it with me as long as it was clean, otherwise I was not interested. He assured me that it was a clean joke, and so he proceeded to tell me the joke. As it turned out the joke was not clean, but he found it very amusing even though he could see that I was not impressed. Something then happened on the inside of me, and I found myself saying the following to him, "because you have shared this joke with a child of God that was not clean, even though I asked you not to share a dirty joke with me, I will now play the next game with you and you will not get one point off of me. I will beat you with a whitewash". I had no doubt that this is exactly what would happen. My friend then really began to laugh, because he knew our comparable games. And so the game began. The first point fell to me and he laughed even more. The second point fell to me and he still laughed, but not so convincingly this time. As each point fell to me he became quieter, and at the end of the game when I had beaten him eleven nil, he was completely astounded and shaken. He went to church with me that weekend for the first time ever (even though I had invited him on many occasions previously). I would like to say that he gave his heart to the Lord that weekend when the altar call was given, but he did not. We have both since moved on and I no longer have contact with him. I do not know whether he has subsequently given his heart to the Lord, but I do know that the Holy Spirit convicted him that day on that squash court. The Holy Spirit manifested the gift of faith through me on that occasion. I must emphasize that this was not my faith. I did not say what I said as an act of

Special faith

exercising my faith, I did not have the kind of faith to do that, this was all God. If it had been my faith I could have gone on to becoming the league champion. But the very next game we played, we got back into our old routine of me barely getting two points off of him. That is what the gift of special faith is. It is God's faith manifested through us as He wills.

Chapter 3
Gifts of healings

Healing by faith

Mark 16:17-18 "And these signs will follow those who believe: In My name, they will cast out demons; ... they will lay hands on the sick, and they will recover."

And so we come to the second of the power gifts listed, which is called the gifts of healings. Before we look at this particular gift however, we need to recognise that scripture reveals two main methods that the Lord uses to heal the sick. The two methods are; healing through the prayer of faith and healing through the spiritual gift called "gifts of healings". In this section we will discuss the first method of healing, i.e. healing through the prayer of faith. In the above quoted passage of scripture we see that the Lord Jesus has mandated all believers to lay their hands on the sick so that they can be healed. And so we see that it is entirely scriptural for all believers to lay their hands on those who are sick, and in faith, pray for them to be healed. In this passage there are three further truths that we learn about this method of healing. Firstly, we see that the sign of healing will follow the one who believes. In other words the outcome of healing is more reliant on the faith of the one who is praying, rather than the faith of the one being prayed for. Secondly, if you read the full context of this passage you will see that the Lord is mandating this method of healing to be used on individuals, not multitudes. The third truth

Gifts of healings

that is revealed in this passage is that in most instances when individuals are healed by this method they will not be instantly healed, for the scripture says that "they will recover", thus implying that they will recover from their illness over a period of time.

> *James 5:14-15 "Is anyone among you sick? Let him call for the elders of the church, and let them pray over him, anointing him with oil in the name of the Lord. (15) And the prayer of faith will heal the sick, and the Lord will raise him up. And if he has committed sins, he will be forgiven."*

In the above quoted passage of scripture the apostle James reinforces the truth to us, that believers can pray in faith for people to be healed and that God will heal them. In this passage the Holy Spirit gives us further insight into this method of healing, for we see that in the church, elders are encouraged to lay their hands on the sick to heal them. So why is that? The reason is because under normal circumstances the elders of the church should be operating at a greater level of faith than the average church member, and should therefore be able to offer this type of prayer more affectively. And so again we see that the outcome of this method of healing is more reliant on the faith of those who are doing the praying, rather than the faith of the one being prayed for. Another truth that is reinforced in this passage is that the Lord encourages the elders to use this method to pray for individuals not multitudes. As an aside, this passage reveals two further facets to this method of healing. Firstly, we see that oil can be used along with the laying on of hands? So why is that? The reason is to help the individual receive their healing as they feel the oil on their bodies and associate that with the healing anointing of the

Gifts of healings

Holy Spirit. Secondly, we see that as far as believers are concerned, unforgiven sin must be dealt with before they can receive their healing. This point is not applicable to unbelievers however.

> Acts 28:8 *"And it happened that the father of Publius lay sick of a fever and dysentery. Paul went in to him and prayed, and he laid his hands on him and healed him."*

The above quoted passage of scripture is an example of this method of healing taking place, for we see the apostle Paul laying his hands on an unbeliever, praying the prayer of faith and healing him. We know that it was Paul's faith that healed this man, because Paul had just arrived on the island and this man, being sick with a fever and knowing nothing about Pauls' healing ministry, could not have exercised any faith of his own to be healed. And so this passage again confirms the truth to us that the outcome of this method of healing is more reliant on the faith of the one doing the praying, rather than the faith of the one being prayed for. The second truth that is reinforced in this passage is the fact that the Lord uses this method to heal individuals not multitudes.

> 2 Timothy 4:20 *"Erastus stayed in Corinth, but Trophimus I have left in Miletus sick."*

We have made an important observation in this section, which is that the outcome of this method of healing is more reliant on the faith of the one doing the praying, rather than the faith of the one being prayed for. Nevertheless as with most spiritual truths, there are exceptions to this rule. The above quoted passage of

Gifts of healings

scripture is an example of one of the exceptions. The context of this passage is that the apostle Paul informed Timothy that he had left Trophimus, who was part of his ministry team, sick in the town of Miletus. As we have already seen in the previous passage of scripture, Paul certainly had the faith to lay his hands on people and pray for them to be healed and they would be healed. So if Paul had that ability why, with one of his own ministry team members being sick, did Paul not just lay hands on him and pray so that he could be healed. The answer lies in the fact that Trophimus was one of Paul's ministry team members, who had travelled and ministered extensively with him. In other words Trophimus was a mature believer, and it is for that reason that Paul's faith proved to be ineffective in this instance. And so the exception we see from this account is that the Lord expects mature believers to exercise their own faith to receive their healing, and not rely on the faith of others. For whatever reason, Trophimus was not able to appropriate his own healing by the time Paul left however, which is why Paul was forced to leave him in Miletus to recover.

Mark 6:5-6 "Now He could do no mighty work there, except that He laid His hands on a few sick people and healed them. (6) And He marveled because of their unbelief."

We have mentioned that there are exceptions to the rule that this method of healing, i.e. healing through the prayer of faith, is more reliant on the faith of the one doing the praying, rather than the faith of the one being prayed for. The above quoted passage of scripture is another example of one of the exceptions. The context of this passage is that the Lord Jesus was preaching the gospel in

Gifts of healings

His hometown of Nazareth. If you read the full account in scripture you will see that this was the one and only time that Jesus preached in Nazareth, because after hearing Him preach, the citizens of that town tried to kill Him by throwing Him off a cliff. Nevertheless the point that I wanted to focus on for the purpose of this discussion, is that this passage declares that Jesus was unable to perform any significant healings in that town. So why is that? It certainly wasn't because Jesus lacked the faith to heal them. The answer lies in the comment that Jesus "marvelled because of their unbelief". We are not talking about weak faith or even neutral faith i.e. the person being prayed for neither believing nor disbelieving. But rather we are talking about unbelief. In other words these people are convinced that they cannot be healed through the laying on of hands. And so the exception we see from this account is that unbelief prevents both the unsaved (and immature believers) from being healed, even if the one who lays hands on them has the faith to heal them. And so we have seen in this section that all believers can practice the method of healing using the prayer of faith. This method does not involve the spiritual gifts of healings however; it is purely the saint laying their hands on a sick individual in faith in order to heal them.

Healing by the anointing

Matthew 10:1 "And when He had called His twelve disciples to Him, He gave them power over unclean spirits, to cast them out, and to heal all kinds of sickness and all kinds of disease."

Gifts of healings

In this section we will discuss the second method of healing, i.e. healing through the spiritual gift called "gifts of healings". One who has this gift is specifically anointed by the Holy Spirit to heal the sick. So what does that mean? It simply means that they are carriers of God's healing power, and anyone who comes into contact with them can potentially draw on that healing power and be healed. And so as we will see in this chapter, the outcome of healing using this method is the opposite to the prayer of faith, because it is more reliant on the faith of the one being prayed for, rather than the faith of the one who is doing the praying. Another difference with this method of healing is that unlike healing through the prayer of faith, this method quite often administers healing through the transference of God's tangible healing power. That truth is revealed to us in the above quoted passage of scripture, for in this passage we see that when our Lord sent out the twelve to cast out demons and heal all kinds of sickness and disease, that He gave them power to do so. So just how did our Lord give the disciples power? If you study scripture you will see that prior to this event the disciples never laid hands on any sick people to be healed, they had only watched Jesus doing that. So what happened on this occasion that convinced the disciples to go out on their own to lay hands on the sick to be healed, having never done so before? The answer lies in the transference of tangible healing power. When Jesus laid his hands on each one of the disciples on this occasion they would have experienced His power flowing into their hands to be able to minister to the sick. Jesus ministered to the sick by the anointing, and He gave that self-same anointing to the disciples. And so having experienced God's tangible healing power being imparted to them, they knew that they were anointed to go out and minister that same power to the sick. It is important to note however, that even though

Gifts of healings

individuals who have this gift carry God's tangible healing power, the same hindrances to healing that take place through the prayer of faith also hinder healing taking place through the operation of this gift. In other words unbelief will prevent both the unsaved (and immature believers) from being healed through the method, even if the one who lays hands on them has the gifts of healings operating through their ministries. Secondly, as far as believers are concerned, unforgiven sin must be dealt with first before they can receive their healing through this method. This point is not applicable to unbelievers however. And thirdly, the Lord expects mature believers to exercise their own faith to receive their healing, and not rely on this gift to receive their healing.

Purpose of this gift

Acts 8:5-8 "Then Philip went down to the city of Samaria and preached Christ to them. (6) And the multitudes with one accord heeded the things spoken by Philip, hearing and seeing the miracles which he did. (7) For unclean spirits, crying with a loud voice came out of many who were possessed; and many who were paralyzed and lame were healed. (8) And there was great joy in that city."

Unlike healing through the prayer of faith, which is really only effective in a one on one situation, saints who have received the spiritual gift called "gifts of healings" are able to minister healing to multitudes at one time. That truth is confirmed to us in the above quoted passage of scripture, where we see that Philip the evangelist was able to heal multitudes of lame and paralysed people in his

Gifts of healings

meetings. The reason for that is because even though it is the same healing power, the amount of healing power made available through the operation of this gift is greatly increased. Another truth that we learn from this passage is that unlike the prayer of faith where very often the sick recover over a period of time, because there is more healing power made available through the ministry of the gifts of healings, this method of healing more often than not results in instant healings taking place. So why does the Lord want this gift to be displayed in the church? As this passage declares, the reason is so that people will be open to the preaching of the gospel when they observe the miraculous healings that take place through the operation of this gift.

Scriptural examples

Acts 28:8-9 "And it happened that the father of Publius lay sick of a fever and dysentery. Paul went in to him and prayed, and he laid his hands on him and healed him. (9) So, when this was done, the rest of those on the island who had diseases also came and were healed."

The above quoted passage of scripture is a classic example of how this gift operates. We quoted this passage earlier to show how the apostle Paul administered healing to Publius' father using the prayer of faith. Nevertheless as we can see, the account doesn't end there, for this passage teaches us that when word got out about Paul's ability to heal the sick, the rest of those on the island who had diseases also came to be healed. Paul knew that he was anointed with the gifts of healings and was therefore not at all pressured when the multitudes came to him to be

Gifts of healings

healed, for he knew that the Holy Spirit would use him in that manner. The only hindrance that prevents the unsaved from receiving their healing through this method is unbelief. Clearly there was no unbelief present on this occasion, because this passage implies that all who came to Paul were healed.

Acts 8:5-8 "Then Philip went down to the city of Samaria and preached Christ to them. (6) And the multitudes with one accord heeded the things spoken by Philip, hearing and seeing the miracles which he did. (7) For unclean spirits, crying with a loud voice came out of many who were possessed; and many who were paralyzed and lame were healed. (8) And there was great joy in that city."

The second example of the operation of this gift which we will discuss is recorded in the above quoted passage of scripture. In this account we see Philip the evangelist going down to the city of Samaria to preach the gospel. If you read the full account in scripture you will see that Philip conducted numerous meetings over a period of time in that city. As with Paul, Philip knew that he was anointed with this gift specifically to heal those who were lame and paralysed. Nevertheless in order for the gift to be able to operate, Philip would have needed to administer healing one on one using the prayer of faith first. And only after successfully healing one or two individuals using that method would word have gone out that Philip could heal the sick. As word got out, more and more people then came to his meetings to be healed by him. Unlike in Paul's case however, this passage declares that many (not all) were healed under Philip's ministry. And so it is evident that even though many were healed that there must still have

Gifts of healings

been a degree of sceptism present, which therefore prevented everyone from being healed.

> *Matthew 4:23-24 "And Jesus went about all Galilee, teaching in their synagogues, preaching the gospel of the kingdom, and healing all kinds of sickness and all kinds of disease among the people. (24) Then His fame went throughout all Syria; and they brought to Him all sick people who were afflicted with various diseases and torments, and those who were demon-possessed, epileptics, and paralytics; and He healed them."*

The gift of healings is highly sought after, and so when someone is identified as having this gift their reputation quickly spreads as more and more people come to be healed. In the above quoted passage of scripture we see that truth confirmed to us, for this passage declares that because Jesus' reputation for healing the sick went throughout Syria, multitudes came to Him to be healed. There is another aspect to this particular phenomenon, which is that as the person's reputation for healing spreads, the expectation for healing increases. In other words the faith of those coming for their healing is strengthened, as they hear of more and more incidents of healing taking place through the individual who has this gift. We see that particular truth also confirmed in this passage, for it is implied that because of His reputation to heal the sick, all who came to Jesus were healed.

> *Mark 5:25-34 "Now a certain woman had a flow of blood for twelve years, (26) and had suffered many things from many physicians. She had spent all that she had and was no better, but rather grew*

Gifts of healings

worse. (27) When she heard about Jesus, she came behind Him in the crowd and touched His garment. (28) For she said, "If only I may touch His clothes, I shall be made well." (29) Immediately the fountain of her blood was dried up, and she felt in her body that she was healed of the affliction. (30) And Jesus, immediately knowing in Himself that power had gone out of Him, turned around in the crowd and said, "Who touched My clothes?" (31) But His disciples said to Him, "You see the multitude thronging You, and You say, 'Who touched Me?' "(32) And He looked around to see her who had done this thing. (33) But the woman, fearing and trembling, knowing what had happened to her, came and fell down before Him and told Him the whole truth. (34) And He said to her, "Daughter, your faith has made you well. Go in peace, and be healed of your affliction."

One who operates in the gifts of healings is specifically anointed by the Holy Spirit to heal the sick, which means that they are carriers of God's healing power. And so potentially anyone who comes into contact with them can draw on that healing power and be healed. The above quoted passage of scripture is a very good illustration of this principle. Our Lord Jesus was anointed by the Holy Spirit with the spiritual gifts of healings (Acts 10:38). And so He constantly carried God's healing power wherever He went. In this passage we see that the woman with the flow of blood touched our Lord's clothes, and the moment she did that the healing power that our Lord was carrying flowed out of Him into her body and instantly healed her. So what caused God's healing power to flow from Jesus into her body. It was her action of faith, for the scripture says that she heard about Jesus. In other words this woman had

Gifts of healings

heard about Jesus' power to heal the sick, but more specifically she had heard about the tangible healing power that flowed out of Him even when one just touched His clothes (Luke 6:19). Because she believed what she had heard, she was fully convinced that if she just touched the Lord's clothes that she too would be healed. And so we see that the Lord Jesus had nothing to do with this incident of healing except to be the conduit for God's healing power to flow through Him into her body. From this account we can clearly see that unlike the method of healing using the prayer of faith, the outcome of this method of healing is more reliant on the faith of the one receiving healing, rather than the faith of the one being used to heal, for on this occasion Jesus' faith was not involved at all.

Acts 5:14-16 "And believers were increasingly added to the Lord, multitudes of both men and women, (15) so that they brought the sick out into the streets and laid them on beds and couches, that at least the shadow of Peter passing by might fall on some of them. (16) Also, a multitude gathered from the surrounding cities to Jerusalem, bringing sick people and those who were tormented by unclean spirits, and they were all healed."

The above quoted passage of scripture is another illustration of the principle that the outcome of this method of healing is more reliant on the faith of the one receiving healing, rather than the faith of the one being used to heal. In this instance we see that the apostle Peter was so anointed by the Holy Spirit, that just his shadow falling on the sick as he walked past them would cause them to receive their healing from the Lord. In other words Peter was not praying for these individuals; he was just walking

Gifts of healings

past them. So why did this phenomenon occur? The same principle applied here as with the Lord Jesus. Word got out that Peter was anointed to heal the sick, and as his reputation spread, more and more people came to him expecting to be healed. Eventually the faith levels were so high in Peter's anointing to heal, that even his shadow touching people was enough to trigger their faith to be activated thus drawing on the healing power that Peter was carrying. There can be no doubt that when this gift is fully manifested that the incidents of healing can be truly phenomenal, both in power and in scope.

Guidelines for this gift

Acts 5:14-16 "And believers were increasingly added to the Lord, multitudes of both men and women, (15) so that they brought the sick out into the streets and laid them on beds and couches, that at least the shadow of Peter passing by might fall on some of them. (16) Also, a multitude gathered from the surrounding cities to Jerusalem, bringing sick people and those who were tormented by unclean spirits, and they were all healed."

Unlike healing through the prayer of faith which all saints can practice, healing through the spiritual gift called "gifts of healings" can only be practiced by those to whom this gift is imparted. So the question is asked, which saints qualify to receive this gift from the Holy Spirit? The first category of saints that qualify are apostles, for one who is called by the Lord to stand in that office will have all nine of the spiritual gifts operating in their ministry, which would include the gifts of healings. That truth is revealed to us in

Gifts of healings

the above quoted passage of scripture, for this passage clearly demonstrates to us that this gift operated through the Apostle Peter's ministry. The apostle Paul's ministry is confirmation of this truth, because there is also clear scriptural evidence that the gifts of healings operated in his ministry (Acts 19:11-12). One of the reasons that the Lord gives this gift to His apostles is so that the church can identify them as such, for Paul speaks about the signs of an apostle being displayed through signs and wonders and mighty deeds (2 Corinthians 12:12). The second category of saints that qualify for this gift are evangelists. The only scriptural example we have of an evangelist is Philip, and if we look at his ministry we can clearly see that the gifts of healings operated through his ministry (Acts 8:5-8). The main reason that the Lord gives this gift to His evangelists, is to demonstrate the reality of God's power to unbelievers so that they can believe the gospel and be saved (Luke 10:9). The third category of saints that can receive this gift are the ministries of the prophet, pastor and teacher. Unlike apostles and evangelists however, this gift is not an essential part of their ministries, and so will only be imparted to certain individuals as the Spirit wills. The fourth and final category of saints that can receive this gift are normal saints. Nevertheless because this gift attracts so much attention, it is rare for this gift to be manifested among the normal saints. The best scriptural example we have of this truth is Stephen. Stephen was an ordinary disciple who had been appointed as a deacon in the church in Jerusalem, and yet the scripture teaches us that through faith and power he performed great signs and wonders among the people (Acts 6:8). The signs that Stephen would have performed would have been miraculous healings, and the reason that Stephen was able to perform those signs

Gifts of healings

was because he was anointed with the spiritual gifts of healings.

>Acts 8:5-8 *"Then Philip went down to the city of Samaria and preached Christ to them. (6) And the multitudes with one accord heeded the things spoken by Philip, hearing and seeing the miracles which he did. (7) For unclean spirits, crying with a loud voice came out of many who were possessed; and many who were paralyzed and lame were healed. (8) And there was great joy in that city."*

All the gifts of the Spirit operate at differing levels of anointing. The highest level of anointing for the gifts of healings is allocated to the office of the apostle, for it is only in that office that we see scriptural accounts of both a one hundred percent success rate and all manner of sickness being healed, e.g. Peter in Jerusalem (Acts 5:16) and Paul in Malta (Acts 28:9). Nevertheless I want you to notice that this gift is called gifts (plural) of healings (plural). So what does that mean? It simply means that outside of the office of apostle, the Holy Spirit anoints the rest of the saints who receive this gift with specific healing power for specific ailments. For example, some are anointed to heal blindness, while others are anointed to heal people who are paralyzed, etc. In the above quoted account in scripture we see Philip being used to heal paralyzed and lame people. There can be no doubt that there were blind and deaf people in the crowds at Philip's meetings, but the bible mentions nothing about them being healed. The reason for that is because Philip was not anointed in that area, for he was anointed to heal those who were paralyzed and lame. And so we see that when it comes to operating in this particular gift, it is very important that the saint knows what anointing they have

Gifts of healings

received from the Lord. For those who recognise where their anointing lies are able to more easily exercise their faith in the operation of their gift, for each one receives ministry gift faith according to the measure of the gift that they have received from the Holy Spirit (Romans 12:3).

> *1 Thessalonians 5:19-21 "Do not quench the Spirit. (20) Do not despise prophecies. (21) Test all things; hold fast what is good."*

In the above quoted passage of scripture the apostle Paul teaches us to test all spiritual gift manifestations to ensure that we are being exposed to the genuine and not the counterfeit. The gifts of healings however, is the one spiritual gift that Satan and his demons cannot counterfeit. So why is that? The reason is because God is the one who endues His creations with power (Psalm 62:11), and in this current dispensation the only creations of God who have been endued with power are the angels, which would include Satan and his angels. Because mankind has not been endued with any power in this age, they are therefore reliant on accessing one of two power sources that are available in this world. The first source is God and His angels, and the second source is the devil and his angels. And so while the saints have access to God's power; the sorcerers have access to Satan's power. The problem that sorcerers encounter in the area of healing however is that while God has endued the devil and his demons with the power to cause sickness and disease (Acts 10:38), He has not endued them with the power to heal. That truth is clearly illustrated to us in the encounter that Pharaoh's magicians had with Moses. Because they had access to demonic power, Pharaoh's sorcerers were able to perform some of the same miracles that Moses performed. However,

Gifts of healings

when Moses caused boils to break out on the Egyptians, not only were the sorcerers powerless to heal the boil outbreak, they were also powerless to prevent the boils from infecting their own bodies (Exodus 9:8-11). And so we see that when the gifts of healings is manifested in the church that it is the genuine gift and not a demonic counterfeit.

    I will close off this chapter with an example this gift operating through my ministry. A number of years ago I was teaching a bible lesson in a morning meeting and after the lesson I invited people who needed healing to come forward for prayer. Among those who came forward for prayer there was a woman who was completely deaf in her left ear. She had been deaf in that ear since she was a little girl due to some incident that had occurred. When I spoke with her I knew in my spirit that she had faith to receive her healing, and so I told her that the moment I laid hands on her that God would heal her. I placed my finger in her ear and prayed for her healing in Jesus name. The moment I did that there was like a small static electric spark that left my finger and went into her ear, and God instantly healed her ear and gave her perfect hearing. She was obviously ecstatic at having been healed, but this incident did not end there. After the Lord healed her I knew in my spirit by revelation of the Holy Spirit, that Satan would try to take her healing from her and so I told her that when she left the meeting that Satan would come and try to steal her healing. In other words I gave her a word of knowledge. I then said that when he did this that all she was to do was to rebuke him in Jesus name and claim her healing, and that her healing would then come back to stay. In other words I gave her a word of wisdom. The following week she stood up in the meeting to testify as to what happened. She said that as she was lying in bed with her husband on the night that she was healed, that she went completely deaf in that ear once

Gifts of healings

again. She said to her husband, not to worry because the preacher had told her this would happen and that all she had to do was rebuke Satan for trying to steal her hearing in Jesus name, and that her hearing would return. She promptly did that, and instantly her healing returned and she has been healed in that ear ever since. And so, we see that in ministry very often the gifts of the Spirit operate together. In this case three gifts of the Spirit were made manifest, the gifts of healings (the Holy Spirit healed her ear), the word of knowledge (the Holy Spirit told her what would happen) and the word of wisdom (the Holy Spirit told her what to do in the situation).

The working of miracles

Chapter 4
The working of miracles

Miracles defined

John 5:19-21 "Then Jesus answered and said to them, "Most assuredly, I say to you, the Son can do nothing of Himself, but what He sees the Father do; for whatever He does, the Son also does in like manner. (20) For the Father loves the Son, and shows Him all things that He Himself does; and He will show Him greater works than these, that you may marvel. (21) For as the Father raises the dead and gives life to them, even so the Son gives life to whom He will."

And so we come to the third of the power gifts listed, which is the gift called the working of miracles. In order for us to have a clearer understanding of this particular gift we need to look at the ministry of the Lord Jesus. Many of the Old Testament prophets operated in the gift of the working of miracles, some examples of which were recorded for us in the Old Testament. And so when the Lord Jesus ministered on the earth He used their recorded miracles to perform similar miracles in His ministry, which is why Jesus said in the above quoted passage of scripture that He did in like manner that which the Father showed Him. There are a number of examples in scripture that we can look at to confirm this particular truth. For example Jesus walked on water, just as Elisha had caused an iron axe head to float on water (2 Kings 6:5-7). Another example would be Jesus feeding the multitudes with a few loaves and having

The working of miracles

some left over, just as Elisha had fed one hundred men with a small quantity of food and having some left over (2 Kings 4:42-44). Another example is Jesus raising the dead, just as Elijah had raised a young boy from the dead (1 Kings 17:17-23). Another example is Jesus turning water into wine, just as Moses had turned water into blood in one of the judgements he pronounced on Egypt (Exodus 7:19). And so these are just some examples to show us that Jesus looked at the miracles that His Father had performed through the prophets in the Old Testament, and in a similar manner He then performed those same miracles in His ministry.

>   Luke 11:20-22 *"But if I cast out demons with the finger of God, surely the kingdom of God has come upon you. (21) When a strong man, fully armed, guards his own palace, his goods are in peace. (22) But when a stronger than he comes upon him and overcomes him, he takes from him all his armor in which he trusted, and divides his spoils."*

We have seen thus far that in similar manner, Jesus performed all of the miracles recorded under the Old Covenant. Nevertheless there is one miracle that Jesus performed which is not recorded in the Old Testament, which is the miracle of casting out demons. So the question is asked, if the Old Testament prophets performed every miracle that Jesus did, why didn't they cast out demons? The Lord Jesus answers that question for us in the above quoted passage of scripture. The context of this passage is that Jesus had just finished casting a mute demon out of someone, thus enabling the person to speak. In trying to explain the miracle that our Lord performed, some of His religious critics accused Him of casting out demons through the use of satanic power. Jesus responded to their

The working of miracles

accusation by explaining that Satan cannot cast out Satan, but that rather it is the power of God that casts Satan's demons out of people. Jesus then went on in this passage to explain why He was able to cast out demons, by giving us the analogy of a strong man being overcome by one who is stronger than him, thus allowing the stronger man to divide the spoils of his weaker enemy. In this analogy the strong man is Satan and the stronger man is Jesus. Therefore we see that because Jesus has overcome Satan, He is able to plunder Satan's kingdom, which would include casting Satan's demons out of people. Under the New Covenant Jesus has given His saints the authority to cast out demons in His name (Mark 16:17). And so we see that because the Old Testament prophets never had access to the name of Jesus, they were unable to perform the miracle of casting out demons.

John 14:12 "Most assuredly, I say to you, he who believes in Me, the works that I do he will do also; and greater works than these he will do, because I go to My Father."

Included in the works that our Lord Jesus did were both gifts of healings and the working of miracles. If you compare the works that our Lord did and the works that the Holy Spirit has done through the church, you will find that there have been no healings greater than that which our Lord performed and neither have there been any greater miracles than that which our Lord performed. There may have been equal, but none greater. The reason for that is because our Lord has taught us that a servant can be like his master but not greater (John 13:16). Nevertheless, in the above quoted passage of scripture our Lord Jesus has taught us that under the New Covenant that we would not

The working of miracles

only do the same works which He did, but that we would also do greater works. So what are the greater works that Jesus is referring to in this passage of scripture? The key to understanding what the greater works are, is in His linking that statement to the words, *"because I go to My Father"*. In other words these works could not be performed in the earth until Jesus had been raised from the dead and had ascended to the Father.

Romans 10:9 "that if you confess with your mouth the Lord Jesus and believe in your heart that God has raised Him from the dead, you will be saved."

And so we see that although Jesus performed similar miracles to the prophets of the Old Testament and He also performed the new miracle of casting out demons, there are nevertheless two miracles which Jesus could not perform while He was on the earth. The first miracle which we will discuss is the miracle of the new birth. Because Jesus had not yet died for our sins and been raised from the dead, He could not get anyone born-again, for as revealed in the above quoted passage of scripture the requirement that must be met to be born-again is to confess Jesus as Lord and believe that God has raised Him from the dead. No-one could do that while Jesus was on the earth. The miracle of the new birth is far greater than any healing or miracle performed by the Lord Jesus, because the miracle of the new birth is an eternal work. And so we see that getting someone born-again is one of the greater works that our Lord Jesus was referring to.

John 7:37-39 "On the last day, that great day of the feast, Jesus stood and cried out, saying, "If anyone thirsts, let him come to Me and drink. (38) He who

The working of miracles

believes in Me, as the Scripture has said, out of his heart will flow rivers of living water." (39) But this He spoke concerning the Spirit, whom those believing in Him would receive; for the Holy Spirit was not yet given, because Jesus was not yet glorified."

The second miracle which we will discuss is the miracle of the saints being filled with the Holy Spirit. This is another miracle that our Lord Jesus could not perform while He walked the earth, for as revealed in the above quoted passage of scripture, it was only after our Lord was raised from the dead that Jesus received the promised Holy Spirit from the Father to pour out on His church. To be filled with the Holy Spirit is also an eternal work, for the Holy Spirit remains with us for all eternity, which makes it a greater miracle than those which Jesus could perform while He walked the earth. And so we see that in the church age that we are able to do the greater works that our Lord spoke about, because Jesus has gone to the Father. The church is able to get people born-again and filled with the Holy Spirit. Both of these works fall into the category of the gifts of the Spirit called the working of miracles, for a miracle occurs when one is born-again and a miracle occurs when one is filled with the Holy Spirit.

Miracles by faith

2 Corinthians 5:18 "Now all things are of God, who has reconciled us to Himself through Jesus Christ, and has given us the ministry of reconciliation."

Before we look at the gift of the working or miracles we need to recognise that just as with the gifts of healings,

The working of miracles

scripture also reveals two main methods that the Lord uses to work miracles through His saints. The two methods are; working miracles through the prayer of faith and working miracles through the spiritual gift called "working of miracles". In this section we will discuss the method of working miracles through the prayer of faith, and the first miracle which we will discuss is the miracle of the new birth. When someone is born-again that is a display of the working of miracles, for it is only by God's power that a new spirit is created in the individual who is born-again (2 Corinthians 5:17). In the above quoted passage of scripture we see that the Lord Jesus has given all believers the ministry of reconciliation. In other words all believers are called to witness to the unsaved around them so that they can believe the gospel and thus be born-again. And so we see that when the saints lead new converts in the sinner's prayer, they are in fact operating in the working of miracles, for in that moment the Lord creates new spirits in those who are born-again. It is important to note however that the ministry of reconciliation given to the saints is for one on one ministry and not for ministering to multitudes.

> *Acts 9:17 "And Ananias went his way and entered the house; and laying his hands on him he said, "Brother Saul, the Lord Jesus, who appeared to you on the road as you came, has sent me that you may receive your sight and be filled with the Holy Spirit."*

The second miracle which we will discuss in this section is the miracle of the saints being filled with the Holy Spirit. When someone is filled with the Holy Spirit that is a display of the working of miracles, for it is God's power that is imparted to the individual who is baptised with the Holy

The working of miracles

Spirit (Acts 1:4-8). Part of the "great commission" that Jesus gave to all His disciples in Mark's gospel (Mark 16:15-18), is that they would speak in new tongues. In other words the Lord mandated all His disciples to be baptised with the Holy Spirit. Nevertheless if you read that statement in context with the rest of the passage you will see that just as all disciples are mandated to proclaim the gospel, heal the sick and cast out demons, so it is also implied that all disciples are also to pray for fellow disciples so that they can be filled with the Holy Spirit. In the above quoted passage of scripture we see that truth confirmed when the Lord used Ananias, who was just an ordinary disciple, to baptise the apostle Paul with the Holy Spirit. And so we see that all saints, that are themselves filled with the Holy Spirit, can lay hands on fellow believers so that they too can be filled with the Holy Spirit. When believers do this they in fact operating in the working of miracles, but again it is important to note that this mandate is given to the saints for one on one ministry and not for ministering to multitudes.

Mark 16:17-18 "And these signs will follow those who believe: In My name, they will cast out demons."

The third miracle which we will discuss in this section is the miracle of casting demons out of those who are oppressed by them. The act of casting out demons is a display of the working of miracles, for it is only by the power of God that demons can be cast out of someone (Luke 11:20). In the above quoted passage of scripture we see that the Lord Jesus has mandated all believers to cast out demons. And so we see that it is entirely scriptural for all believers to lay their hands on those who are tormented by unclean spirits, and to cast them out using the

The working of miracles

mechanism of the working of miracles. However, if you read the full context of this passage you will see that the Lord is mandating this method of deliverance to be used on individuals and not multitudes, and the reason for that is simple. Not all believers have received the gift of the working of miracles and can therefore only minister to individuals by faith in this area, as and when the need arises.

Miracles by the anointing

> *1 Corinthians 12:8-10 "for to one is given the word of wisdom through the Spirit, to another the word of knowledge through the same Spirit, (9) to another faith by the same Spirit, to another gifts of healings by the same Spirit, (10) to another the working of miracles."*

Just as with the gifts of healings, there are those who have received the gift of working of miracles. These are individuals who are more anointed by the Holy Spirit to operate in the area of the working of miracles. And so one who has received the gift of the working of miracles would experience far more success and be able to minister to far more people than one who performed miracles simply by faith. For example, it is self-evident that those called to the office of the evangelist are anointed to get far more people saved than normal saints witnessing one on one to the unsaved. It is also self-evident that the Lord uses certain ministry gifts, such as apostles and evangelists, to cast out demons on a far greater scale than normal saints ministering one on one to those tormented by demons. It is just as self-evident that the Lord uses certain ministry gifts

The working of miracles

such as apostles and prophets, to baptise multitudes with the Holy Spirit, whereas normal saints are only able to minister one on one to those needing to be baptised. And so we see that in all instances those who operate in the gift of the working of miracles operate in the same anointing as those who operate by simple faith, just in a far greater measure of anointing.

Purpose of this gift

Acts 8:14-17 "Now when the apostles who were at Jerusalem heard that Samaria had received the word of God, they sent Peter and John to them, (15) who, when they had come down, prayed for them that they might receive the Holy Spirit. (16) For as yet He had fallen upon none of them. They had only been baptized in the name of the Lord Jesus. (17) Then they laid hands on them, and they received the Holy Spirit."

The context of the above quoted passage of scripture is that Philip the evangelist had preached the gospel in Samaria, resulting in multitudes being saved. Nevertheless after they were saved Philip did not lay hands on them to be filled with the Spirit. So why is that? The reason is because Philip recognised that he was not anointed in that area. Unlike working miracles through the prayer of faith, which is really only effective in a one on one situation, saints who have received the spiritual gift called "working of miracles" are able to minister to multitudes at one time. That truth is confirmed to us in this passage, for in this passage we see that because Peter and John operated in the working of miracles in this area, they were able to baptise the newly saved multitudes with the Holy Spirit as they laid hands on

The working of miracles

them. The reason for that is because even though it is the same miraculous power, the amount of power made available through the operation of this gift is greatly increased. So why does the Lord want this gift to be displayed in the church? One of the main reasons is practicality, for as the above example shows us, it is far more practical for one who is anointed with this gift to minister to multitudes all at once, rather than having one individual trying to lay hands on each individual in faith to having them filled with the Holy Spirit.

Scriptural examples

Acts 8:5-12 "Then Philip went down to the city of Samaria and preached Christ to them. (6) And the multitudes with one accord heeded the things spoken by Philip, hearing and seeing the miracles which he did. ... (12) But when they believed Philip as he preached the things concerning the kingdom of God and the name of Jesus Christ, both men and women were baptized."

The first example of the working of miracles which we will look at in this section is the miracle of multitudes being born-again. There are two main ministry gifts which the Lord uses to operate in the working of miracles in this area, i.e. apostles and evangelists. Philip is the only example of an evangelist that is given to us in scripture (Acts 21:8). In the above quoted account in scripture we can see clear evidence of the working of miracles taking place through Philip's ministry, for this passage declares that multitudes were baptised in the name of the Lord Jesus as they heeded the things spoken by Philip. And so we see that whenever

The working of miracles

an evangelist preaches the gospel multitudes are born-again, which is a display of the gift of the working of miracles operating through their ministries. As I have already mentioned, this same gift also operates through the ministry of the apostle, for example we see that when Peter and John preached the gospel in the temple that multitudes were born-again in response to their message (Acts 4:1-4).

> *Acts 8:5-7 "Then Philip went down to the city of Samaria and preached Christ to them. (6) And the multitudes with one accord heeded the things spoken by Philip, hearing and seeing the miracles which he did. (7) For unclean spirits, crying with a loud voice came out of many who were possessed; and many who were paralyzed and lame were healed."*

The second example of the working of miracles that we will look at is the miracle of many being delivered from demonic oppression as demons are cast out of them. Again there are two main ministry gifts which the Lord uses to operate in the working of miracles in this area, i.e. apostles and evangelists. In the above quoted account in scripture we can see clear evidence of the working of miracles taking place through Philip's ministry as an evangelist; for this passage declares that many were delivered from demonic oppression as Philip cast the unclean spirits out of them. And so we see that whenever ministry gifts are used by the Lord to cast out demons, it is a display of the gift of the working of miracles operating through their ministries. As I have already mentioned, this same gift also operates through the ministry of the apostle, for example we see that many that were tormented by unclean spirits were healed through Peter's ministry (Acts 5: 16).

The working of miracles

Acts 8:14-17 "Now when the apostles who were at Jerusalem heard that Samaria had received the word of God, they sent Peter and John to them, (15) who, when they had come down, prayed for them that they might receive the Holy Spirit. (16) For as yet He had fallen upon none of them. They had only been baptized in the name of the Lord Jesus. (17) Then they laid hands on them, and they received the Holy Spirit."

The third example of the working of miracles that we will look at is the miracle of multitudes being filled with the Holy Spirit. There is one main ministry gift which the Lord uses to operate in the working of miracles in this area, i.e. apostles. We see that truth revealed to us in the above quoted passage of scripture. The context of this passage is that this is a continuation of the account of the city wide revival that had taken place through Philip's ministry. This passage reveals to us that although multitudes had been born-again and delivered from demonic oppression under Philips ministry, none of the new converts had been filled with the Holy Spirit. The reason for that was because Phillip did not have this particular gift operating in his ministry. Phillip knew that the disciples needed to receive the Holy Spirit, and so he sent to Jerusalem to ask for help in this area. When the apostles heard about Phillip's request, they specifically sent Peter and John to them, and the reason that Peter and John went was because they had the gift of the working of miracles in this area, which as this passage teaches us, enabled them to lay hands on the disciples so that they could be filled with the Holy Spirit.

Acts 20:9-12 "And in a window sat a certain young man named Eutychus, who was sinking into a deep sleep. He was overcome by sleep; and as Paul

The working of miracles

continued speaking, he fell down from the third story and was taken up dead. (10) But Paul went down, fell on him, and embracing him said, "Do not trouble yourselves, for his life is in him." (11) Now when he had come up, had broken bread and eaten, and talked a long while, even till daybreak, he departed. (12) And they brought the young man in alive, and they were not a little comforted."

The fourth example of the working of miracles that we will look at is the miracle of raising the dead. There is one main ministry gift which the Lord uses to operate in the working of miracles in this area, i.e. apostles. In the above quoted account in scripture we see this gift operating through Paul's ministry as he raised Eutychus from the dead. And we have another account in scripture of the apostle Peter raising Tabitha from the dead (Acts 9:39-41). And so we see that although this type of miracle is very powerful it is none the less not manifested very frequently, i.e. we only have two examples given to us in the book of Acts. There are a number of reasons why this miracle is performed very infrequently in the church. One of the reasons is because this miracle can only be performed on children and the Lord's saints, for it is only those individuals that God allows to be raised from the dead, because their spirits ascend into heaven when they die. Whereas unbelievers who die are cast into hell and God does not allow them out, which means that they cannot be raised from the dead.

Guidelines for this gift

The working of miracles

2 Corinthians 12:12 "Truly the signs of an apostle were accomplished among you with all perseverance, in signs and wonders and mighty deeds."

The most common working of miracles in the church age, are getting people born-again, casting out demons and baptising the saints with the Holy Spirit. The reason that these miracles are the most common is because they have the greatest impact on the church. And so although those who are anointed with this gift are also used by the Lord to perform other miracles, i.e. raising the dead, etc, nevertheless scripture shows us that these other miracles are the exception rather than the norm. The main reason for that is because of the limited impact that other miracles have on the church as a whole. Because this particular gift is so powerful, it seems that it is only given to a few, and then only to those who are called to one of the ministry gifts. As revealed to us in the above quoted passage of scripture this particular gift definitely forms part of the Apostle's ministry. Nevertheless we have also seen that this gift forms part of the evangelists ministry, and I'm sure that it can form part of the prophet's ministry as well.

As with the other gifts of the Spirit, I will close this chapter with an account of this gift operating through my ministry. I attended a men's prayer meeting a little while ago and during the meeting a strong spirit of prayer came upon me and I began to pray with great boldness. As I prayed the anointing came into my hands and I recognized it immediately as the anointing for the filling of the Holy Spirit (I have had this anointing upon me many times and it feels like electricity flowing through my hands. Sometimes it is stronger than at other times.) On this occasion I knew that the anointing would not last very long, so I called out

The working of miracles

to all who wanted to be filled with a fresh anointing of the Holy Spirit to come up so that I could lay hands on them. Everyone that came up fell instantly under the power of the Holy Spirit and received a fresh anointing from Him.

The working of miracles

If you believe you can receive Jesus as your Lord and Saviour by praying this prayer

Dear Heavenly Father,

I come to You in the Name of Jesus.

Your Word says, "the one who comes to Me I will by no means cast out" (John 6:37), so I know You won't cast me out, but You take me in and I thank You for it. You said in Your Word, "Whoever calls on the name of the lord shall be saved." (Romans 10:13). I am calling on Your Name, so I know that You save me right now. You also said, "If you confess with your mouth the Lord Jesus and believe in your heart that God has raised Him from the dead, you will be saved. (10) For with the heart one believes unto righteousness, and with the mouth confession is made unto salvation" (Romans 10:9-10). I believe in my heart Jesus Christ is the Son of God. I believe that He was raised from the dead for my justification, and I confess Him now as my Lord. Because Your Word says, "with the heart one believes unto righteousness," and I do believe with my heart, I have now become the righteousness of God in Christ Jesus (2 Cor. 5:21) . . .

And I am now saved!

Thank You, Lord!

Welcome to the family of God. Now that you are His child you need to read your bible (especially the New

Testament) daily, spend time in prayer daily and join a local church that will teach you to be filled with the Holy Spirit with the evidence of speaking in other tongues, so that you can grow spiritually. You also need to tell others how Jesus has saved you so that they too can be saved.

About the Author

From childhood, Michael E.B. Maher has always known that the Lord's call was upon his life for the ministry. When he was saved at the age of twenty-two, almost immediately the Lord Jesus began to deal with him about entering the ministry. However, it was only many years later that he committed to the Lord to answer the Lord's call to the ministry. And so, in 2014 Michael Maher Ministries was begun. From the beginning, the mandate given to Michael from the Lord Jesus was to preach the word. And so, this ministry preaches the word of God on every available platform around the world.

Michael Maher Ministries

Free Subscription

Join hundreds of others from countries around the world and read our Daily Bible Teaching Email and more, that will help you to grow in your walk with the Lord Jesus.

Everyday I look forward to your teaching on God's Word. Keep letting God use you my Brother. I so look forward to seeing all of these things unfold!

- *Lisa Turner*

Amen to keeping on keeping on. Thank you for today's lesson. We must never forget to pray regularly and immerse ourselves in the Word – "a page (or Chapter) a day helps keep Satan at bay".
Blessings,

- *John Lombard*

Thank you so much for today's inspiration. This made so much sense to me and helped me overcome a huge block in my understanding.
Blessings and love

- *Pam Laughton*

Log on to our website to subscribe.

www.mebmaher.wixsite.com/website

Michael Maher Ministries

Online Bible Courses

Our courses are designed to help believers grow in their faith and reach their full potential in Christ that God intended for their lives, through the study of His word.

Flexible

Enrol any time: choose your topic of study; study at your own pace.

Affordable

Pay as you go.

Log on to our website to register.

www.mebmaher.wixsite.com/website

Michael Maher Ministries

46 Penguin Road
Pringle Bay, 7196
South Africa
Phone: +27 082-974-3599

On the Web

www.mebmaher.wixsite.com/website